P9-CLC-299

The Girl with a

Story by
EWA ZADRZYNSKA

Illustrations by
ARNOLD SKOLNICK

Paintings from the
NATIONAL GALLERY OF ART
WASHINGTON, D.C.

CHAMELEON BOOKS, INC.
New York

Watering Can

Published by Chameleon Books, Inc.
211 West 20th Street
New York, New York 10011

Text copyright © 1990 by Ewa Zadrzynska
Illustrations copyright © 1990 by Arnold Skolnick
Compilation copyright © Chameleon Books Inc.

All rights reserved. No part of this book may be
reproduced or transmitted in any form or by any
means, electronic or mechanical, including
photocopying, recording, or by an information
storage and retrieval system, without permission
of the publisher.

Designed by Arnold Skolnick
Edited by Marion Wheeler
Typography by MGL Graphics, New York
Printed and bound by O.G. Printing Productions, Ltd., Hong Kong

ISBN #0-915829-64-9

Auguste Renoir, 1841-1919
A Girl with a Watering Can, 1876
Oil on canvas, 39½ x 28¾ in.
Chester Dale Collection

Since 1870, the Girl with a Watering Can has been standing quietly in her garden in a painting by the French artist Pierre-Auguste Renoir, which now hangs in the National Gallery of Art in Washington, D.C.

Suddenly, one night, for apparently no reason at all, the Girl with a Watering Can sat down on the garden path, took off both her shoes, and said to herself, "The stupid stone in my left shoe has been hurting me for a long, long time."

Once her shoes were off, anything seemed easy. She wiggled her toes in her very clean white socks and jumped out of the painting, carrying her watering can but leaving her shoes and bouquet behind.

She looked back at her garden and saw the color disappearing. But she didn't care because, in the painting next to her own, called *Girl with a Hoop*, she saw another French girl. She, too, had been painted by Pierre-Auguste Renoir, but in 1885.

"Oo-la-la. I have a friend at last," the Girl with a Watering Can said softly, and she came closer to get a better look at her neighbor.

"I am the daughter of a very important French senator, and I choose my friends very carefully," the Girl with a Hoop said. "Who is your father?"

"I don't know," said the Girl with a Watering Can, and she grabbed the hoop right out of the stuck-up girl's hand.

"Help! Help!" the senator's daughter shouted, as all the color in her painting disappeared, too. But there was no one to hear her, because the museum had been closed for hours and everyone had gone home.

The hoop slipped from the Girl with a Watering Can's hand, fell to the floor, and rolled into the next room.

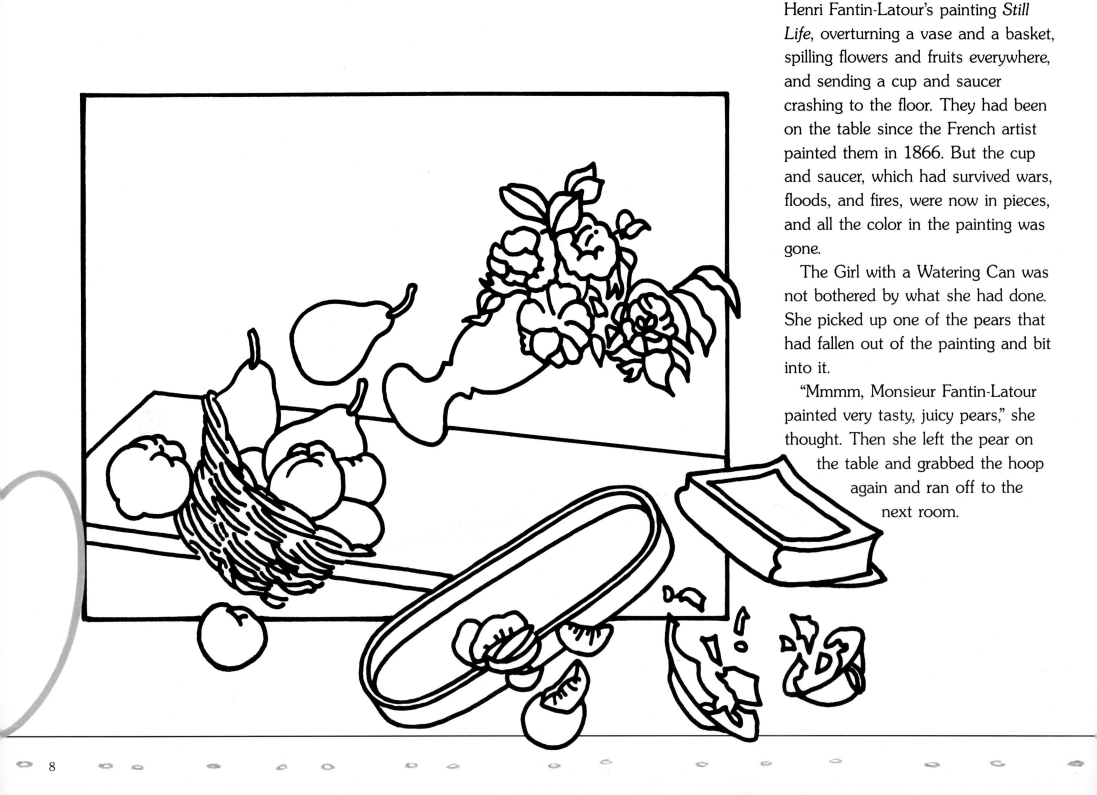

The hoop bumped into a table in Henri Fantin-Latour's painting *Still Life*, overturning a vase and a basket, spilling flowers and fruits everywhere, and sending a cup and saucer crashing to the floor. They had been on the table since the French artist painted them in 1866. But the cup and saucer, which had survived wars, floods, and fires, were now in pieces, and all the color in the painting was gone.

The Girl with a Watering Can was not bothered by what she had done. She picked up one of the pears that had fallen out of the painting and bit into it.

"Mmmm, Monsieur Fantin-Latour painted very tasty, juicy pears," she thought. Then she left the pear on the table and grabbed the hoop again and ran off to the next room.

There the Girl with a Watering Can saw *The Equatorial Jungle.* Henri Rousseau, another French artist, had painted this jungle in 1909, and the two monkeys he had painted in the middle of it were still living there.

"I have never been in a jungle before," she thought. "I wonder what it's like."

Boldly, she climbed into the jungle and sat down next to the monkeys. She looked around and began to laugh.

"This is not a jungle. Monsieur Rousseau has deceived you," she said to the astonished monkeys, while all the green around them was fading. "These are just ordinary potted plants."

The Girl with a Watering Can picked up a small fern in a pot and dropped it, scattering soil everywhere. When the monkeys began to chatter, she jumped out of the painting.

From somewhere nearby, she heard PUFF-CHUG, PUFF-CHOO. A train was about to pull into the Gare Saint-Lazare, a train station in Paris, painted by Edouard Manet.

The Girl with a Watering Can grabbed hold of the fence outside the station and pulled herself into the painting. There she met a girl whose golden hair was neatly tied up with a black ribbon. The golden-haired girl has been waiting for the same train to come into the Gare Saint-Lazare since 1883. In just a minute, it will arrive and the passengers will get off. That minute has lasted for more than 100 years.

"Come on!" the Girl with a Watering Can shouted to the golden-haired girl. "You are wasting your time. The train will never come. It is Monsieur Manet's train. Only he can make it come into the station, and he doesn't want it to. You would have a lot more fun if you came and played with me."

The golden-haired girl did not turn her head, but she said primly, "I do not want to play with naughty girls."

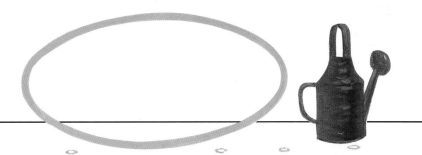

The Girl with a Watering Can reached out and pulled the black ribbon very hard, and the girl's hair tumbled down her back. The little brown-and-white dog, who had been asleep on the governess's lap, woke up and barked as his spots began to disappear. Just as he was about to bite the Girl with a Watering Can, she leaped out of the painting and picked up the hoop. She gave it a push, and it rolled away from her onto the banks of the Thames River in a painting called *Mortlake Terrace* by an English artist named J. M. W. Turner.

The Girl with a Watering Can ran after the hoop. That is how she found herself in England on a sunny afternoon with a small group of people who were watching boats drift down the river.

"Have you seen my hoop, by any chance?" she asked a woman standing beside a big tree.

"There is no hoop here," the woman answered.

"But I saw my hoop roll into this painting," the Girl with a Watering Can insisted.

"I have been here since 1827, and I have never seen any hoop. Wait a minute," said the woman. "You are the Girl with a Watering Can. You ask about 'your' hoop. Since when do *you* have a hoop?"

When the Girl with a Watering Can didn't answer her, the woman said, "I know. You stole it from the Girl with a Hoop." Then the woman shouted to her friends, "This girl is a thief! Catch her!"

The Girl with a Watering Can ran as fast as she could to the edge of the painting, which had just lost its color. She jumped out, picked up her watering can, and ran into the next room.

There she stopped in front of *Self-Portrait* by Judith Leyster, a Dutch painter, who was holding a paintbrush in one hand and a palette in the other.

"Why are you so happy?" she asked the woman in the painting.

"Why shouldn't I be happy? I am the first famous woman painter in the world. There were very few of us in the seventeenth century, and I was the best."

"I want to paint, too," exclaimed the Girl with a Watering Can, and, without asking, she grabbed the palette. It was hard to balance, and it slipped out of her hand and fell with all the brushes onto the floor. The Girl with a Watering Can ran away and didn't look back. She didn't even see that all the color had left the painting.

The Girl with a Watering Can stopped this time in front of *Breezing Up*, which was painted by the American artist Winslow Homer in 1876. In it, a man and three boys were sailing far out to sea with the wind at their backs.

"Let me show you how to sail into the wind," she cried.

But the wind was picking up and nobody heard her.

"I bet you are too scared to sail into the wind," she said and knocked the hat off the boy near the rudder. At the same time all the color left

the painting. Just before the hat fell out of the painting, the boy reached for it. The boat almost keeled over, and the sail touched the water. The boys held on to the sides of their colorless boat, while the skipper shouted angrily at them.

By that time, the Girl with a Watering Can was already far away at the circus, standing in front of *Bareback Riders* painted by the American painter W. H. Brown in 1876.

"How exciting," she said to herself. "They all look like they are flying. Even the horse! I want to fly, too."

But when she jumped into the ring, she brought the frightened horse down to earth, upsetting the bareback riders' perfect balance.

"Hey, what are you doing here?" the clown cried out. "You'd better get out of here quick."

The Girl with a Watering Can took one look at the angry ringmaster shaking his whip, and she fled, taking the color with her.

Almost out of breath, the Girl with a Watering Can stopped in front of Giovanni Bellini's beautiful painting *St. Jerome Reading*. When she reached out to close the book that the old man in the cave had been reading for more than 500 years, she lost her balance and fell into a hole right in front of him.

The hole was a very dark and very unpleasant place to be. The Girl with a Watering Can tried to get out, but she slipped back. She tried again, but again she failed. The hole was too deep, too narrow, and too slippery to climb out of without help.

"But who will help me now, after I've caused so much trouble?" she thought. "I spoiled the Bareback Riders' performance. I knocked off the boy's hat, and the sailors' boat almost capsized. I took the lady painter's palette and dropped it on the floor. I made the girl's hair messy at the Gare Saint-Lazare, and I told the monkeys in *The Equatorial Jungle* that their jungle wasn't real. The Girl with a Hoop doesn't have a hoop anymore because of me, and the people in *Mortlake Terrace* think I am a thief. How will I ever get out of this hole?" The Girl with a Watering Can began to cry.

St. Jerome looked up from his book and peered into the hole. "Why have you been so naughty?" he asked.

"It is Monsieur Renoir's fault. He put the stone in my shoe," the Girl with a Watering Can said between sobs.

"Well, my child, a stone in your shoe, no matter who put it there, does not mean that you can do as you please and cause trouble for others," St. Jerome said solemnly.

"But the stuck-up Girl with a Hoop refused to be my friend because I don't know who my father is," the Girl with a Watering Can protested.

St. Jerome shook his head. "Even if the senator's daughter did not want to be your friend, that does not give you the right to be inconsiderate of others."

"Oh, I know that," said the Girl with a Watering Can. "But I was just so happy to see the Girl with a Hoop, right after I got that nasty stone out of my shoe, that I didn't think about anything at all except being her friend. When I couldn't be her friend, I took the hoop, and, when it rolled away I just followed it."

"Ah, yes," said St. Jerome gently, "you followed it and did what?"

The Girl with a Watering Can sighed a big sigh. "I guess I did do some naughty things. But now I am very sorry that I did them. I didn't mean to cause any trouble. Please believe me and help me to get out of this terrible hole so I can go back to my garden."

"I will help you, my child," St. Jerome replied, "but only on one condition: You must promise me that you will go back to each painting and apologize for all the naughty things you have done, and that you will put everything back just as it was."

Giovanni Bellini, ca. 1427-1516
Saint Jerome Reading, ca. 1480/1490
Oil on wood, 19¼ x 15½ in.
Samuel H. Kress Collection

21

W. H. Brown, active 1886/1887
Bareback Riders, 1886
Oil on cardboard, 18½ x 24½ in.
Gift of Edgar William and Bernice Chrysler Garbisch

"I will, I will," the Girl with a Watering Can promised, and, without another word, St. Jerome reached down and pulled her out of the hole.

And that is how the Girl with a Watering Can found herself once again standing in the National Gallery of Art, not so very far away from where she lived.

"I have no idea how to get back to my garden," she said to herself. And then she noticed a trail of little water drops. Luckily, her watering can had been leaking ever since she left her painting.

Following the trail, The Girl with a Watering Can returned to the Bareback Riders. "I am terribly sorry I spoiled your performance, and I do hope you aren't hurt," she said as she helped them both to their feet. She gently stroked the horse as first the man and then the woman climbed onto his back. The Girl with a Watering Can waved goodbye and slipped out of the painting. When the Bareback Riders had regained their perfect balance and the horse's hooves lifted above the floor of the ring, the painting regained all its vivid color.

The Girl with a Watering Can felt very proud of herself as she left the Bareback Riders and approached *Breezing Up*. She picked up the hat and put it back on the boy's head.

"I'm sorry I knocked off your hat," she said as loud as she could. "I don't really know how to sail into the wind," she added. No one in the boat could hear her, because the wind was still blowing very hard. But, suddenly, the sail lifted out of the water and the painting brightened with color.

Winslow Homer, 1836-1910
Breezing Up (A Fair Wind), 1876
Oil on canvas, 24⅛ x 38⅛ in.
Gift of the W. L. and May T. Mellon Foundation

The Girl with a Watering Can went next to Judith Leyster's *Self-Portrait* and found the palette on the floor where she had left it. Fortunately, it had landed right side up. She gathered up all the brushes and arranged them neatly on the palette before she handed it back to the artist.

"I'm sorry I took your paints and brushes and dropped them. I think the painting you are working on is very, very good," said the Girl with a Watering Can. The artist smiled and color flooded the painting.

Judith Leyster, 1609-1660
Self-Portrait, ca. 1635
Oil on canvas, 29⅜ x 25⅝ in.
Gift of Mr. & Mrs. Robert Woods Bliss

The Girl with a Watering Can paused between two rooms in the museum. She knew that she should go to *Mortlake Terrace* to get the hoop that she had taken from her neighbor, the Girl with a Hoop. But, because she was afraid that she would have trouble getting it back, she went instead to the *Gare Saint-Lazare*. She climbed into the painting and quickly found the ribbon that she had so carelessly dropped. She very carefully tied it around the girl's hair so that it looked just as it had before.

The golden-haired girl said, "I know that the train will never come into the station, but I like the sound that it makes, PUFF-CHUG, PUFF-CHOO. Don't you want to stay here and listen to it with me?"

"I do, but my place is in my garden," the Girl with a Watering Can replied.

The golden-haired girl nodded and said politely, "It was nice to meet you. I hope to see you again some time."

When the Girl with a Watering Can left the painting, the color returned. The little dog, happy to have his lovely brown spots again, went back to sleep.

Edouard Manet, 1832-1883
Gare Saint-Lazare, 1873
Oil on canvas, 36¾ x 43⅞ in.
Gift of Horace Havemeyer
in memory of his mother, Louisine W. Havemeyer

By now, the Girl with a Watering Can was very tired. All she wanted to do was to climb back into her garden, but the watchful eyes of the monkeys in the colorless *Equatorial Jungle* reminded her of her promise to St. Jerome. She marched right up to the painting and set the potted fern upright in its place and put back all the soil in the pot she had spilled. The jungle was as brilliantly green as before.

The Girl with a Watering Can then told the monkeys that their jungle of potted plants was ever so much more beautiful than any real jungle and that they should not be ashamed of it at all.

Henri Rousseau, 1844-1910
The Equatorial Jungle, 1909
Oil on canvas, 55¼ x 51 in.
Chester Dale Collection

Henri Fantin-Latour, 1836-1904
Still Life, 1866
Oil on canvas, 24⅜ x 29½ in.
Chester Dale Collection

Wearily, the Girl with a Watering Can went into the room where the flowers, fruits, cup, and saucer from Henri Fantin-Latour's painting *Still Life* were lying on the floor in front of it. She picked them up and set them back on the table. With great patience, she put all the pieces of the cup and saucer together. To her happy surprise, they stuck together. Then, she turned the side of the pear she had bitten toward the wall. The moment she finished, the flowers brightened and color glowed everywhere in the painting.

Now, with great apprehension, the Girl with a Watering Can reluctantly returned to J. M. W. Turner's painting *Mortlake Terrace*. She saw the hoop right away. It was leaning against a wall near the riverbank very close to the edge of the painting. But, when she climbed up to the edge and reached in to pick it up, the people nearby saw her and shouted, "Stop thief! Stop thief! Catch her! Catch her!"

When she fled without the hoop, Mr. Turner's famous light and color returned to the riverbank, but she was too upset to notice.

Joseph Mallord William Turner, 1775-1851
Mortlake Terrace, ca. 1826
Oil on canvas, 36¼ x 48¼ in.
Andrew W. Mellon Collection

"What ever will I do now?" the Girl with a Watering Can cried out in frustration. "St. Jerome will be so angry with me. The Girl with a Hoop will never get her hoop back, and I will probably have to live in a garden without color for ever and ever."

"Come in here, and I will lend you my brush to paint a new hoop," a familiar voice called from a room nearby.

The Girl with a Watering Can rushed back to Judith Leyster's *Self-Portrait* and gratefully accepted the brush that the painter offered her. She carried it into the room where she and the Girl with a Hoop lived, taking great care to make sure that no paint dripped onto the floor. She walked up to the *Girl with a Hoop* and, without a word, painted her a brand-new hoop. For just a moment, the bright gold of the hoop was the only color in the painting. Then there was color everywhere.

Auguste Renoir, 1841-1919
Girl with a Hoop, 1885
Oil on canvas, 49½ x 30⅛ in.
Chester Dale Collection

The Girl with a Watering Can returned the brush to Judith Leyster. "Thank you so much for your help," she said. "I would love to stay and talk to you about painting pictures, but I really have to get back to my garden."

"Go," Judith Leyster said, "and you will find your garden as beautiful as it was before you left it."

So it was that the Girl with a Watering Can, who was very, very tired after her many adventures, climbed back at last into her own painting, which was indeed just as beautiful as before.

Since that night, she has been standing quietly in her garden, wearing her high-buttoned shoes. Smiling slightly, she holds a watering can in one hand and a bouquet of flowers in the other.

The hoop that she left in Mr. Turner's painting *Mortlake Terrace*, is still there, leaning against a wall near the riverbank, very close to the edge of the painting. If you doubt it, go to the National Gallery of Art in Washington, D.C. and take a look for yourself.

Auguste Renoir, 1841-1919
A Girl with a Watering Can, 1876
Oil on canvas, 39½ x 28¾ in.
Chester Dale Collection

The ten paintings in the National Gallery of Art, Washington, D.C., reproduced in this book are:

Auguste Renoir, 1841-1919
A Girl with a Watering Can, 1876
Oil on canvas, 39½ x 28¾ in.
Chester Dale Collection

Auguste Renoir, 1841-1919
Girl with a Hoop, 1885
Oil on canvas, 49½ x 30⅛ in.
Chester Dale Collection

Henri Fantin-Latour, 1836-1904
Still Life, 1866
Oil on canvas, 24⅜ x 29½ in.
Chester Dale Collection

Henri Rousseau, 1844-1910
The Equatorial Jungle, 1909
Oil on canvas, 55¼ x 51 in.
Chester Dale Collection

Edouard Manet, 1832-1883
Gare Saint-Lazare, 1873
Oil on canvas, 36¾ x 43⅞ in.
Gift of Horace Havemeyer
in memory of his mother, Louisine W. Havemeyer

Joseph Mallord William Turner, 1775-1851
Mortlake Terrace, ca. 1826
Oil on canvas, 36¼ x 48¼ in.
Andrew W. Mellon Collection

Judith Leyster, 1609-1660
Self-Portrait, ca. 1635
Oil on canvas, 29⅜ x 25⅝ in.
Gift of Mr. & Mrs. Robert Woods Bliss

Winslow Homer, 1836-1910
Breezing Up (A Fair Wind), 1876
Oil on canvas, 24⅛ x 38⅛ in.
Gift of the W. L. and May T. Mellon Foundation

W. H. Brown, active 1886/1887
Bareback Riders, 1886
Oil on cardboard, 18½ x 24½ in.
Gift of Edgar William and Bernice Chrysler Garbisch

Giovanni Bellini, ca. 1427-1516
Saint Jerome Reading, ca. 1480/1490
Oil on wood, 19¼ x 15½ in.
Samuel H. Kress Collection